Helga looked at the sky.

"Something's coming this way," she said.

"We'd better head home."

Erik quickly pulled

his fishing line from the stream.

He was only seven,

two years younger than Helga.

But he knew the prairie.

The land was flat.

Storms were violent and sudden.

"I've never seen a sky
like that before," said Erik.
"There's something shiny in those clouds."
"I don't like it," said Helga.
"I hope Father's back from town.
This is going to be a terrible storm."

Helga and Erik walked farther.

The great white cloud turned a smoky gray
and crept closer.

"What's that noise?" asked Erik.

Helga listened.

She could hear a strange deep hum.

"Hurry," said Helga. "It could be a tornado."

As they walked faster,
darkness swept over the sky.
In minutes, day turned to night,
and a buzzing, sawing sound
moved above them.
Then suddenly, the cloud swooped down.
Hail-like objects dropped to the earth,
striking their faces and hands.
"Run!" screamed Helga. "RUN!"
A dark swarm surrounded them.
The noise was ear-splitting.
Small brown crackling bodies
squirmed through their hair
and down their shirts.
Helga and Erik scraped the clawing insects
off their clothes
as they streaked across the field.

Minutes later,

the sky was cloudless.

The warm summer sun shone.

Helga and Erik stopped running.

They couldn't believe their eyes.

They were ankle-deep

in a sea of *grasshoppers*!

Grasshoppers were everywhere.

Some were flying.

Some were hopping.

The cornfield was in a crunching uproar!

"Look," said Helga.

"All the stalks are bent to the ground."

"They're eating all the corn!" cried Erik.

Just then,

they heard a racket in the distance.

"Mother needs help," cried Helga.

"Let's go."

Helga bolted ahead.

Erik dashed after her.

They raced through the cornfield,

hoppers squishing under their bare feet.

Soon they could see their mother.

She was clanging pots and pans together.

"Nothing will scare them away,"

Mrs. Lundstrom yelled.

"Help me save the garden."

She handed her children

some bedsheets and blankets.

Helga shook off the grasshoppers

from a tomato plant

and quickly covered it.

But seconds later, the hoppers

wriggled their way underneath.

"It's no use," said Helga.

"They're going under the sheet."

"And they're eating the green blanket

you gave me," said Erik.

"Then pull out as many vegetables

as you can," shouted Mrs. Lundstrom.

At that moment, a shot rang out.

A brown cloud billowed up in a cornfield.

Helga spotted the family's wagon.

"It's Father," she cried.

"He's shooting at the grasshoppers."

Mr. Lundstrom raced his team of horses
into the yard.

"Get the lantern!" he shouted.

Helga and her mother ran to the sod house.

When they stepped inside,

Mrs. Lundstrom screamed.

Helga looked across the room and gasped.

A blanket of grasshoppers

was covering her baby sister, Etta!

Mrs. Lundstrom rushed to the cradle,

scooped up the crying infant,

and brushed off the hoppers.

"Take the lantern to your father,"

she told Helga. "Hurry!"

Helga dashed outside to her father.

She found him digging a trench.

She had never seen him so angry.

"Help your brother," he said loudly.

"Get something we can burn."

Helga rushed to Erik's side

and swept her hands

under the mass of hard brown bodies.

Together, the children searched

for grass and twigs.

It wasn't easy.

The scratching hoppers kept jumping

onto their arms and backs.

But finally, an hour later,

they had filled the ditch.

Now their father could set

the grass and twigs ablaze

and shovel in the grasshoppers.

For a moment, the fire burned wildly.

But grasshoppers kept hopping

into the trench by the hundreds.

Soon the hoppers had smothered the flames.

In minutes, the fire was out.

At first, everyone was speechless.

Then Helga cried out,

"Fire won't kill them. Now what do we do?"

"I don't know," said her father.

"But there's nothing more we can do today.

We'd better go help your mother."

Mrs. Lundstrom

was still clutching the baby

when they entered the soddy.

"They're everywhere," she moaned.

"On the floor, in the beds."

Mr. Lundstrom slid his shovel

along the floor

and lifted up a load of hoppers.

"Come," he said to Helga and Erik.

"Take the brooms and shovels.

We'll find every last one and get them out!"

When the last hoppers had been swept out,
they closed the door and the shutter.
Then the family ate what little food
the grasshoppers had not attacked.
Mr. Lundstrom spoke of his trip to town.
"News is, the grasshoppers have taken over
the entire area.
They're eating everything in their path."
Mr. Lundstrom pushed his plate aside.
"No one knows what to do."

That night, no one slept much.

Helga stayed awake for hours.

She prayed the grasshoppers would go away.

But the next morning,

the grasshoppers were still there.

And when the family checked the barnyard,

they found the chickens

staggering in the clutter of insects.

"The fool animals," said Mr. Lundstrom.

"They've eaten too many grasshoppers."

"Everything smells so awful," said Erik.
Mr. Lundstrom drew a bucket of water
from the well.

"YUCK," said Helga.

"They're in the well."

"Even our water supply!" cried her father.

"Have they left us nothing!"

He handed Helga and Erik each a bucket.

"Help me with these.

We'll go to the stream."

Things were no better at the stream.

"Look what they did," cried Helga.

"The water is brown, and it stinks!

What will we drink?"

Mr. Lundstrom shook his head.

"We'll go back to the well.

Maybe we can clear out the hoppers

and cover it so no more get in.

Then when we get a rainstorm,

we can catch the rain in buckets."

They went back to the well
and used their buckets
to scoop out the water mucked up
by hoppers and their smelly droppings.
Then Helga's father built a trap.
First, he made a shallow pan
from a long sheet of metal.
He placed a large screen behind the pan.
He put two boards under the pan
for runners.
Then he hitched the trap behind a horse
and filled the pan with kerosene.
The children helped guide the horse
across the fields.
When the trap passed by,
the hoppers hit the screen
as they jumped up.
When they fell into the pan, they died.

But there were too many grasshoppers.
The Lundstroms would never be able to kill
the millions of insects on their land.
Their only hope now
was to find some crops
that the hoppers might have spared.

For the next six weeks,
they spent each day searching the fields.
And they did have some luck.
They found enough food to keep them fed.
But they didn't find enough crops to sell.

The days passed.

The longer the hoppers stayed,

the harder life became.

One morning, Helga's mother looked out

the soddy window.

"Many people are giving up," she said.

"There goes another wagon."

"Where are they going?" asked Helga.

"Maybe they have folks back East,"

said her mother.

"Will we leave too?" Helga asked.

"We will never leave," said her father.

"We have put too much time

and work into this land to quit."

He raised his hands in the air.

 "This is our home now.

Besides, we have no money.

We cannot go back to Sweden."

Two weeks later,
as they walked across the stripped fields,
Mr. Lundstrom spoke to his family.
"The grasshoppers have gone.
But they have left their eggs in the soil."
"The eggs could never live
through a Minnesota winter,"
said his wife.

"They might," said Mr. Lundstrom.

"Things could be worse next spring."

Helga's mother cradled the baby.

"How will we live?" she asked.

"We have lost ten acres of wheat,

five hundred cabbage,

and all cucumbers, beans,

onions, carrots, and beets."

"At least we have enough to eat
for a while," said Mr. Lundstrom.
"Some oats, corn, potatoes, and tomatoes."
Mrs. Lundstrom handed Helga the baby.
"But we have no money," she said.
"We needed the wheat crop to sell.
We need money to buy feed for the animals
and seed for next year's crop.
We need fabric to make clothes.
I've patched things as much as I can."

Mr. Lundstrom reached for his wife's hand.

"There's only one thing to do.

I must leave and find work."

"Oh, no!" cried Helga's mother.

"You can't leave us here alone."

"I must," said Helga's father.

"I can get a good job up north.

The lumber camp at Stillwater needs men."

"Can't we go with you?" asked Helga.

"No. You must stay here," he said.

"We will lose our land if we all leave.

And it's your job to see

that the animals live through the winter."

For the next four weeks,
Helga's father spent the time hunting,
and her mother kept busy
salting and smoking the meat.
Then the day came
when Mr. Lundstrom had to leave.
Everyone felt sad and afraid.

But there was no time for tears.
"We must prepare for winter,"
Mrs. Lundstrom said to her children.
"You two take the wheelbarrow.
Spend this week
looking for firewood and cow chips.
We'll put everything in sacks
and stack it in a corner of the house."

Helga knew what to do.
"Let's go to the stream,"
she told Erik.
"We can always find driftwood there."
As they walked,
they looked for cow chips—
chunks of dried dung
left by grazing herds of cattle.

"Look," said Erik,

when they reached the stream.

"The grasshoppers are gone,

and the water is clean.

We can go fishing again."

Helga smiled.

The thought of having fish to eat again

lifted her spirits.

"Maybe things will get better."

The next few weeks passed slowly.

When the weather was good,

Helga and Erik walked a mile to school

at Mrs. Hale's house.

But winter soon closed in.

Helga began to dread the nights.

In the darkness,
she worried about her father.
The lumber camp is a dangerous place,
she thought.
Father could be crushed by a falling tree.
She worried that he might get killed,
and they'd be stuck alone in the wilderness.

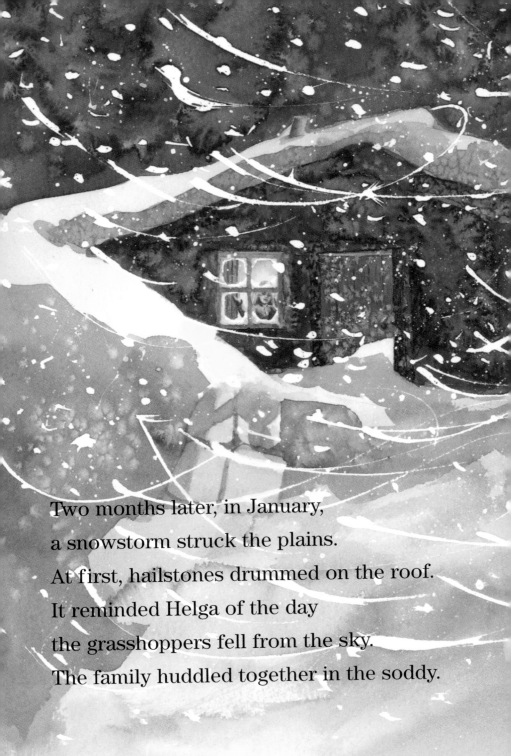

Two months later, in January,
a snowstorm struck the plains.
At first, hailstones drummed on the roof.
It reminded Helga of the day
the grasshoppers fell from the sky.
The family huddled together in the soddy.

I wish we were with Father, thought Helga.
I'm tired of being here without him.
I'm tired of being cold.
I'm tired of cornmeal.
The wind howled.
The blizzard raged all night.

The next morning, Mrs. Lundstrom
shook Helga awake.
"Come, Helga. The storm has ended.
We must go to the barnyard."
While Erik stayed with the baby,
Helga helped her mother
shovel a path to the barn.
then they carried a kettle of hot water
to melt the ice in the animals' trough.
It was cold—too cold to be outdoors.
But Helga remembered her father's words.
"It is your job to see
that the animals live through the winter."

The winter seemed endless.

But finally, three months later,

Helga's father returned home.

He was just in time to see

the grasshopper eggs hatching.

Everyone waited to see what would happen.

They hoped the crops would be spared.

But for weeks,
the pests feasted in the fields.
Then in July,
the young insects grew wings.
This time, the Lundstroms were lucky.
The grasshoppers did not lay eggs
on their farm.

One day,

Helga and Erik were at the stream.

"Look," said Helga, pointing to the sky.

Little dark whirlwinds swirled above them.

The sky grew thick with clouds.

Then the sun was blotted out.

The grasshoppers were flying away.

They left the way they came.

Author's Note

This fictional story is set in the southwestern prairie area of Minnesota. Between 1873 and 1877, millions of Rocky Mountain locusts (grasshoppers) invaded Canada and the midwestern and plains states from Montana to Texas. Hardest hit were parts of Minnesota, the Dakotas, Kansas, Nebraska, Iowa, and Missouri.

Some farmers lost most of their crops for several years. Others experienced little damage, or severe damage only once.

The people of the plains states were a determined group. Some were originally from the South and New England. Some were from Sweden, Norway, and Germany. During the grasshopper plagues, some settlers were helped by relatives back East, who sent money and clothes. But many farmers did not have relatives to help them. For these people, hard work and courage were the only things that pulled them through these difficult times.

These farmers received little help from the rest of the country. The government gave the farmers small amounts of cash and seed. But this did not go far. The seed was only enough for planting a few acres of crops.

Selling their animals would not help. The farmers needed their cows and horses to plant a new crop and care for their families.

Even without the grasshopper attacks, prairie life was difficult. Trees were scarce. So homes were often built of bricks made from blocks of dirt and grass, or sod. Where available, sun-dried cow and buffalo droppings were used for fuel. Prairie life also meant dealing with wild animals, snakes, tornadoes, fires, drought, hailstorms, and blizzards.

Although there was another series of grasshopper plagues in the 1930's, destruction by grasshoppers has declined in the United States. But grasshoppers are still a serious problem for farmers and ranchers. Many people continue to study ways to control this pest.